The

Senior's Guide
to Easy Computing

PC Basics, Internet, and E-Mail
Updated!

The

Senior's Guide
to Easy Computing

PC Basics, Internet, and E-Mail
Updated!

By Rebecca Sharp Colmer

EKLEKTIKA PRESS
Chelsea, Michigan

To Flip

"When the student is ready, the Master appears."
Buddhist Proverb

ACKNOWLEDGMENTS

Thanks to:

Flip Colmer, who worked every bit as hard on this book as I did. Thanks for your assistance, inspiration and encouragement. You are still the best!

Thanks to:

Malcolm Colmer, Ruth Bell, Tim Zulewski, Ron Steblea, Vera Doyle and Samara Anjelae.

Table of Contents

Introduction

- Why Own A Computer?   15
- Why Should You Use This Book?   16
- Objectives And Limitations   17
- I Want To Hear From You   18

Understanding PC Basics

- What Is A Personal Computer?   19
- Why Should I Have A PC?   20
- Is A Mac (Apple Macintosh) a PC?   21
- Types Of PCs   22
- What Is Hardware?   23
- What Is A "Propeller Head"?   24
- What Is Software?   25
- What Are Applications?   26
- What Is An Operating System?   27
- What Is The Central Processing Unit (CPU)?   28
- What Is CPU Speed?   29
- What Is Random Access Memory (RAM)?   30
- What Is A Megabyte?   31
- Ram Vs. Hard Drive Storage   32
- What Are Disk Drives?   33
- How Do Drives Differ?   34
- What Is A Floppy Drive?   35
- What Is The Hard Drive?   36
- What Is A CD-Rom Drive?   37
- What Is A Monitor?   39

Table of Contents

- What Is A Qwerty Keyboard?   40
- What Is A Mouse?   41
- What Are Expansion Slots?   42
- What Is Multimedia?   43
- What Is A Printer?   44
- What Is DPI?   45
- What Is A Modem?   46
- What Is Baud Rate?   47
- Is Modem Speed Important?   48

Getting Set-Up
- How Do I Get Started?   49
- Picking The Best Workspace   50
- Connections   51
- Turning On The PC   52

Understanding Windows
- What Is The Windows Operating System?   54
- What Is The Desktop?   55
- What Is The Taskbar?   56
- What Is An Icon?   57
- What Is A Pointer?   58
- What Is The Difference Between
    The (A:), (C:), and (D:) Drives?   59
- What Is A File?   60
- What Is An Extension?   61
- What Is A Folder?   62

Table of Contents

Start-up/Shut-down

- Booting Up — 63
- What Should I See On The Screen After The Start-Up? — 65
- What Is A Window? — 66
- Recognizing The Parts Of A Window — 67
- What Are The Mouse Functions? — 68
- What Is The Taskbar? — 70
- What Is The Start Button? — 71
- How Do I Shut Down The PC? — 73
- How Do I Re-Start The PC? — 74

Basic Skills

- Basic Skills — 75
- Opening A Window — 77
- Resizing A Window — 78
- Moving A Window — 79
- Too Many Open Windows? — 80
- What Is A Scrollbar? — 81
- What Is A Menu? — 82
- What Is A Menu Bar? — 83
- Using Menus And Sub-Menus — 84
- What Is A Shortcut Menu? — 85
- What Are The Key Functions? — 86
- How Do I Close A Program? — 88

Table of Contents

Windows Tasks

- What Is A Dialog Box?   89
- How Do I Find Files And Folders?   90
- How Do I Open A File or Folder?   91
- How Do I Rename A File Or Folder?   92
- Copying And Moving Files And Folders   93
- How Do I Create A Folder?   95
- Delete Files and Folders   96
- How Do I Customize The Desktop?   97
- How Do I Play A CD?   98
- Playing Sounds   99
- Sound Recorder Toolbar   100
- Playing Media Clips And Movies   101
- What Is A Screen Saver?   102
- How Do I Get A Screen Saver?   103

Programs

- What Is A Program?   104
- Windows Programs   105
- New Programs   106
- How Do I Add A New Program?   108
- How do I Remove A Program?   110
- How Do I Start A Program?   111
- How Do I Quit A Program?   112
- Word Processing Overview   113
- Spreadsheet Overview   114
- Games   115

Table of Contents

- What Is Multitasking?   116
- Using My Computer   117
- Using Windows Explorer   118
- Working With My Documents   119

File Management

- File Management   120
- Backing Up   121
- Hard Disk Maintenance   122

Internet

- What Is The Internet?   124
- Where Did The Internet Originate?   125
- What Is the World Wide Web?   126
- What Can I Do On The Internet?   127
- Who Owns And Runs The Internet?   128
- How Many People Are On The Internet?   129
- Is There Bad Stuff On Internet?   130
- Security On The Internet   131
- What Is Needed To Get Online?   132
- How Do I Get Connected?   133
- What Is An ISP?   134
- Which Online Service Is The Best?   135
- Can I Switch Online Services?   136
- Where Do I Get The Software To Access The Internet?   137

Table of Contents

- What Is A Web Browser? — 138
- How To Choose A Browser — 139
- What Is A Domain Name? — 140
- How Do I Log On To The Internet? — 141
- What Is A Web Page/Web Site? — 142
- What Is A Home Page? — 143
- What Is Hypertext Linking? — 144
- What Is A URL? — 145
- What Is The Meaning Of http? — 146
- How To Surf The Web — 147
- Internet Explorer Toolbar Buttons — 148
- How Do I Search For A Topic? — 150
- Cannot Open A Web Page? — 151
- Web Address Error Codes — 152
- What Is An FTP Program? — 153
- How Do I Download A File From The Web? — 154
- What Is Uploading? What Is Downloading? — 155
- Is There An Easy Way To Return To My Favorite Sites? — 156
- What Is A Newsgroup? — 157
- What Are Chat Rooms? — 158
- What Is A Plug-In? — 159
- What Is A Cookie? — 160
- What Is A Virus? — 161
- Logging Off The Internet — 162

Table of Contents

E-Mail

- What Is E-Mail? 163
- How Does E-Mail Work? 164
- What Do I Need To Get Started? 165
- What Is An E-Mail Address? 166
- How Do I Send E-Mail? 167
- How Can I Be Sure That The Message Was Sent? 168
- How Do I Receive E-Mail? 169
- How Do I Use The Address Book? 170
- Addressing E-Mail Shortcut 171
- How Do I Reply To E-Mail? 172
- How Do I Forward E-Mail? 173
- Sending Carbon Copies And Blind Carbon Copies 174
- How Do I Attach A File To My E-Mail Message? 175
- How Do I Receive Attachments? 176
- Is E-Mail Private? 177
- Reading And Composing E-Mail Offline 178
- Emoticons 179
- E-Mail Etiquette 180
- Acronyms 181

- **101 Hot Tips** 182
- **101 Terrific Web Sites** 198
- **Index** 205

DISCLAIMER

Every effort has been made to make this book as complete and as accurate as possible. However, there may be mistakes both typographical and in content. Therefore, this text should be used as a general guide and not as the ultimate source of computer information.

Trying to keep up with the ever-changing computer technology and the Internet is nearly impossible. If you find something that is not right, please let me know via e-mail.

WHY OWN A COMPUTER?

"Do I really need a computer?" We all asked the same question at the introduction of the first microwaves, VCRs and touch-tone telephones. You are probably thinking that you have gotten along just fine, all of these years, without a computer.

There will soon be a time when having a computer will be as common as having a telephone, and just as necessary.

A computer is a valuable tool and its uses are infinite. For instance, a computer can make it easier and less expensive to communicate with your children and grandchildren. A computer can help you to make new friends and find old friends. Online shopping is easy and convenient: a time and money saver.

Most of all, a computer can help simplify your life so that you have more time to enjoy all your favorite things.

WHY SHOULD YOU USE THIS BOOK?

Ready or not, computers have become the life-blood of modern American society. You would probably agree that access to information is a necessary tool for living. Owning a computer puts the world of information at your fingertips.

We are an aging nation. The first of the 76 million Baby Boomers turned 50 in 1996. Between now and 2030, the aged will become a dominant segment of our population. Many Seniors and Baby Boomers are going online for the first time.

This "user friendly" handbook will help the person who wants the basic facts about using a PC, sending e-mail, and surfing the Internet. It is intended for a novice or new computer user. However, experienced users will find it helpful, too.

As much as possible, this book will try to make your computer experience as easy as possible. "Insert tape. Push play." If only it were that easy!

OBJECTIVES AND LIMITATIONS

Let me make one thing clear right at the beginning. This book is not a textbook on how to learn everything there is to know about computers.

Rather, it is an organized collection of PC, Internet, and e-mail fundamentals.

This is a crash course in "basics". It's simple. It's fun. It will get you going fast!

This book will help you to become computer functional, but not necessarily computer literate. We'll leave the techno-babble to the "propeller heads".

I WANT TO HEAR FROM YOU

Send me your stories about your computer experiences.

Send me your questions.

Tell me about your favorite places in cyberspace.

Go to my web site at **www.theseniorsguide.com**

Or

Send e-mail to **rscolmer@theseniorsguide.com**

Or

Contact me the old fashioned way:
The Senior's Guide
EKLEKTIKA Press
P. O. Box 157
Chelsea, MI 48118

WHAT IS A PERSONAL COMPUTER?

A personal computer is a stand-alone computer that is equipped with a central processing unit (CPU), one or more disk drives, random access memory (RAM), a monitor, a keyboard, and a mouse.

It comes in an assortment of shapes and sizes.

A personal computer is a device that allows you to do a lot of work in a very short amount of time. It allows you to communicate with businesses, friends, family and strangers around the world. It helps you organize all of your information from your personal address book, your checkbook, and your photos if you have a digital camera or a scanner.

Your personal computer will become a teacher of new skills, games, and ideas. Your computer is YOUR personal assistant.

WHY SHOULD I HAVE A PC?

PCs are electronic tools that serve many functions. They can be used for fun or business. The possibilities are unlimited. Here are just a few things you can do with a PC:

- Manage your finances.
- Write letters. Write a book.
- Play the stock market. Make day trades from home.
- Trace your family history.
- Online shopping.
- Pay your bills electronically.
- Meet your friends in a chat room.
- Connect with your kids and grandkids.
- Find old friends.
- Make new friends.
- Debate popular issues.
- Entertain yourself.
- Express yourself artistically.
- Play games such as solitaire, bridge, or chess.
- Digital photography: store, manage or edit.
- Listen to music.
- Watch movies.
- And more.

IS A MAC (APPLE MACINTOSH) A PC?

No. In 1981 IBM introduced a personal computer called the IBM PC. When other manufacturers created computers that worked just like the IBM model, they called them clones or compatibles.

Although the Apple Macintosh (Mac) is small and personal, it uses a different operating system and is not called a PC.

Think of it as the difference between a cassette and audio CD. The result is the same, beautiful music playing for your enjoyment. However, CDs and tapes are not interchangeable due to the different operating systems that run them.

TYPES OF PCs

There are two broad categories of PCs: stay at home and portable.

Home computers come in two basic models, desktop and tower. Due to their size, they are not frequently moved.

The desktop model sits horizontally on your desk while the tower models sits vertically. The tower model has a smaller footprint and takes up less desk space. The orientation of the system box is the only difference in the two computers.

Portable computers such as laptops and notebooks are much smaller and are easily transported. They are lightweight and can sit comfortably in your lap. They run on batteries and connect to household electricity.

Laptops are just as powerful in their computing abilities as desktops; but they cost more.

WHAT IS HARDWARE?

Hardware is a term for the physical components that are included when you purchase a PC. They include the system box, monitor, keyboard and mouse.

You can purchase additional hardware items such as modems, CD-ROM drives, DVD drives, video and digital cameras and whatever else the "propeller heads" invent.

By itself, hardware is not capable of doing anything. Look at your stereo. It sits there looking nice, without emitting sounds until the hardware pieces are given the sounds to play.

Your computer needs something to make it work. That something is software.

WHAT IS A "PROPELLER HEAD"?

A propeller head is a term of endearment I use for those people who create, build or have a hand in the development of all the computer-based technologies that we use today.

In the past, we may have called these folks nerds, geeks, Poindexters or any number of not-so-endearing terms. However, the joke is on us. They are the ones creating all of the latest and greatest technologies for us to use.

WHAT IS SOFTWARE?

Software tells the hardware how to work, what to do, and when to do it.

Software is what gives your computer its identity. It includes the basic operating system, utility, or application programs, all expressed in a language your hardware understands.

There is software to tell your computer to do just about any task. Think about when you first balanced your checkbook. Either someone showed you how to do it or you followed the instructions on the back of your statement. Those instructions "programmed" you on how to do the task at hand: balancing your checkbook.

Those instructions were your "software" and you were the "hardware" that did the work.

WHAT ARE APPLICATIONS?

Software applications are programs that a computer uses so that the machine accomplishes predetermined tasks.

Each application performs a specific kind of work, such as, word processing, desktop publishing, accounting, personal finance, etc.

There is an application for just about any task you can think of. Do you want to organize your stamp collection? There's software to help you do just that. Do you want to design your next home? Yes, software exists for that too.

A utility program is an after-market application that does housekeeping operations to assist you in maintaining and improving your computer's performance.

WHAT IS AN OPERATING SYSTEM?

An operating system is the master control program for the computer. It is the stored information that your computer needs to operate.

Without an operating system all of the hardware would just sit there and collect dust! The hardware is like your skeleton, muscles, and organs. Without a brain you would just sit there and collect dust, too!

WHAT IS THE CENTRAL PROCESSING UNIT (CPU)?

Sometimes we refer to the CPU as the system box or brain. It is the computer chip that does all of the processing for the computer.

Inside this tiny chip are millions of transistors (electrical switches) that are connected so they can carry out mathematical calculations. Everything a computer does is essentially a mathematical calculation.

WHAT IS CPU SPEED?

We measure the central processing unit's (CPU) speed in megahertz (MHz). Megahertz is a unit of measurement commonly used to compare the speeds of computers. These days, so many MHz have been added that we now see gigahertz (GHz) when talking about processor speeds.

The higher the CPU's megahertz/gigahertz rate, the faster it processes information and instructions.

WHAT IS RANDOM ACCESS MEMORY (RAM)?

RAM is the computer's primary working memory.

RAM is used for short-term storage while the computer does its work. It is read/write memory.

RAM is distinguished from ROM, which is read-only memory. The more RAM you have the more your computer can do at one time.

RAM is volatile memory. It needs to be running to "remember" what it is doing. In case of a system failure or power interruption, you will lose all of your work in RAM that you have not saved on a disk drive. Save your work frequently.

WHAT IS A MEGABYTE?

A megabyte is a large unit of measurement of storage capacity. Here is how storage capacity is calculated:

- **Bit** = smallest amount of info.

- **Byte** = eight bits strung together.

- **Kilobyte** (KB or K) = about 1000 bytes.

- **Megabyte** (MB or meg) = about a million bytes.

- **Gigabyte** (GB or gig) = about a billion bytes.

RAM VS. HARD DRIVE STORAGE

Storage is where the program is kept, RAM is where it works.

The amount of space a program needs for storage on the hard drive has nothing to do with how much RAM is needed to run the program.

Many PC programs take up many megabytes of storage space. Many programs also require at least 4MB of RAM or more, to operate efficiently.

To run today's popular programs, make sure your computer has adequate RAM and storage.

WHAT ARE DISK DRIVES?

Disk drives allow you to store and move data from, and to, different types of media.

There are several types of drives: floppy drive, hard drive, CD-ROM drive, and DVD drive, external hard drive, removable drive and portable drive.

Because the computer world is ever changing, expect to see new drives in the future that will run our programs faster and make our tasks much simpler. In the computer world, change is good. However, you do not have to change computers every time a "new" improvement is made.

HOW DO DRIVES DIFFER?

The biggest difference in drives is size or capacity. Drives also differ in how fast they take to find and access information.

WHAT IS A FLOPPY DRIVE?

A floppy disk drive is an economical, removable storage medium. It uses a magnetic disk. You can record or erase it and then remove it from the computer. You can use the removable disk repeatedly.

Today's floppy is 3.5 inches of square, stiff plastic with a magnetic disk inside. It is called a floppy because the original disk, way back when, was large and floppy like a hound dog's ear. The term "floppy" is still with us.

To read or write to a floppy disk, insert the disk into the floppy disk drive slot on the front of your system box.

WHAT IS THE HARD DRIVE?

The hard drive, or hard disk, is your PC's main storage device. It's sometimes called the C:/ drive and pronounced "cee" drive. Data is magnetically stored there. It stores programs and data files.

A typical hard disk holds at least 20 gigabytes of storage.

WHAT IS A CD-ROM DRIVE?

CD-ROMs are compact discs, read-only, removable storage media. CD-ROMs read the data encoded on the disc and then transfer this data to the computer.

CD-ROMs are different from hard drives and floppy disks, in that you cannot store your own information on them.

One CD-ROM can hold as much information as about 450 floppy diskettes.

The RW CD-ROM drive is a re-writeable CD-ROM drive. It allows you to read, erase, and use it repeatedly like a floppy drive.

Not all CD-ROM disks are re-writeable. Some are re-writeable multiple times, some only once and some not at all! Read the label!

WHAT IS A DVD?

DVD stands for digital versatile disk.

DVD drives read DVDs.

A DVD holds about 5 gigabytes of information while a CD-ROM only holds about 700 megabytes.

A CD-ROM drive cannot read a DVD. However, DVD drives can read CD-ROMs.

Soon there will be DVD-RW drives that are easily affordable.

WHAT IS A MONITOR?

Sometimes we call the monitor a CRT (cathode ray tube) and sometimes we refer to it as a video display unit.

The monitor attaches to the video output of the computer and produces a visual display.

Most computers these days come with a 15-inch monitor. For an additional cost you can upgrade to a larger monitor. Large monitors are a dream to work with and make it much easier to view your work. However, they take up more space on your desk.

Flat panel monitors are economically priced and they take up less room on a desk. However, they generally cost more than the same size CRT monitor.

WHAT IS A QWERTY KEYBOARD?

It is the standard typewriter keyboard layout, used for computer keyboards.

It is the most frequently used input device for all computers.

The keyboard provides a set of alphabetic, numeric, punctuation, symbol, and control keys.

WHAT IS A MOUSE?

The mouse is a control device. It controls the pointer on your computer screen.

It is housed in a palm-sized case. When you move it on your desk, the corresponding arrow, commonly known as the pointer, moves on the computer screen.

Think of it as a remote control for your computer. Move the mouse left and right, the pointer moves left and right. Move the mouse forward and backward, the pointer moves up and down the screen. Using the mouse to command the computer to do most tasks can eliminate many keyboard strokes.

The flashing bar, known as the cursor, is where the work will take place on the computer screen. To move the cursor with the mouse, place the pointer where you want the cursor to appear and click the mouse.

One mouse click is one quick press of the left button of the mouse.

WHAT ARE EXPANSION SLOTS?

Your system has expansion slots so you can add additional hardware, known as peripherals or add-ons.

Some slots may already be taken for a sound card or video card.

Expansion cards give the computer additional capabilities.

WHAT IS MULTIMEDIA?

Multimedia is a term used to describe any program that incorporates some combination of sound, music, written text, pictures, animation, and video. Almost all of the computers on the market today are multimedia capable.

WHAT IS A PRINTER?

A printer is a device designed to print your computer-generated documents onto paper. Printers vary in their quality, speed, graphics capabilities, fonts, and even paper usage. There are dozens of brands of printers. The four most popular types of printers are dot matrix, ink jet (bubble jet), laser printers, and photo quality printers.

- **Dot Matrix.** A dot matrix printer uses a print head and a ribbon to print a document. These printers are inexpensive and tend to be slow and loud. Their print quality is fair.
- **Ink Jet or Bubble Jet.** An inkjet printer works by spraying tiny dots of ink onto the paper. The print head controls the spray pattern to form the print. Excellent print quality at a reasonable price.
- **Laser.** A laser printer offers great quality and fast printing. It is also more expensive than the other two types of printers.
- **Photo quality.** A photo quality printer allows you to print your own photographs (from a digital camera) that look just as good as those from a camera store.

WHAT IS DPI?

DPI (dots per inch) is a measure of how good a printer is. The more DPI, the better the print, and the easier it is to read.

WHAT IS A MODEM?

A modem is the communications hardware that allows your computer to send and receive information from other computers, over a telephone line, cable TV line or satellite dish.

Most new computers come with internal modems. If you have an older computer you might have an external modem-a small box with a phone jack connected to your computer.

You will need a modem (and a telephone line, cable line, or satellite dish) to hook up to online services and the Internet.

WHAT IS BAUD RATE?

Baud rate is the number of times a modem's signal changes per second when transmitting data. It is how modem speed is measured. The bigger the number, the faster you can communicate.

The fastest connection is via satellite, then cable, then D.S.L. (Digital Subscriber's Line). Telephone connections are the slowest method.

IS MODEM SPEED IMPORTANT?

Yes. Common speeds for today's telephone modems are between 28,800 and 56,600 kilobytes per second (expressed as 28.8K and 56.6K). The existing telephone lines can only handle up to about 56K.

DSL, cable and satellite modems all have speeds in excess of 56.6. This allows you to download items from the internet much faster.

HOW DO I GET STARTED?

First, you need a computer or at least access to one. You can get access to computers at libraries, schools, recreation centers, cyber-cafes and senior centers, just to name a few places.

If you are still shopping for a computer, get as much information as you can before making the purchase. Be prepared to receive contradictory opinions. Everyone has their own opinion on what is best and what to avoid.

Because computer technology is changing rapidly, make sure you are not buying something that will soon be obsolete. Before making your decision, collect information and advice from friends, family and computer store personnel.

One way to test the water is to borrow some computer time from your kids and grandkids! If you are concerned that you may not need all of the bells and whistles being offered, get a second opinion. For most new computer purchases, it is not necessary to spend thousands of dollars.

PICKING THE BEST WORKSPACE

You will need a flat surface (usually a desk or table), with a nearby power source and telephone, cable or satellite jack. The area should be well lit. Invest in a surge protector. You can plug all the components into the power strip while protecting against power surges.

If you don't have a computer desk (with a keyboard shelf at a good height for typing), be sure you can type comfortably on your keyboard. Your wrists should be flat as you type. If you have to bend your wrists to type you could develop a repetitive stress injury. You can buy an ergonomic keyboard that is designed to lessen muscle stress associated with typing. However, it is more expensive than a regular keyboard. Be sure that you can view the monitor comfortably. Is it too close or too far? Is it at eye level? Is there any glare?

Once you have picked the best workplace, you can unpack your PC. Remember to save the boxes just in case you ever have to ship your computer. Keep the manuals and documentation handy.

CONNECTIONS

Your computer will come with a complete set of instructions on how to set it up. It will tell you what cables need connecting, and to where.

Some manufacturers have even color-coded the connections. For example, red to red, green to green, etc.

It doesn't take a genius to set up a computer. However, it does take some lifting, maneuvering and crawling around. Invite a friend, neighbor, or neighbor's kid over to help you!

There will be a written "quickstart" guide for you to read, even though the detailed instructions about the computer are found in the Help menu.

TURNING ON THE PC

After you make all the connections and plug in the power cord, turn on the power switches or buttons. Generally, both the system box and the monitor have a power switch.

The power switch on the system box is typically located on the front of the machine. You should see an indicator light go on to let you know the machine is on.

The power switch for the monitor is usually located on the front panel. There will be other adjustment buttons on your monitor to fine-tune the picture, just like on your TV.

If you are using a surge protector, follow closely the instructions in your operations manual.

Always follow the prescribed shut down procedures for your computer. You should not just turn it off. You should wait until the software is ready to turn off. Once it says to turn it off, you can use your surge protector master switch.

It is not the end of the world if you shut down improperly. You may get some extra messages cautioning you not to "do that again".

There will be times when your computer will crash or freeze-up for no apparent reason. DON'T PANIC! It is the nature of computers to get confused every once in awhile.

WHAT IS THE WINDOWS OPERATING SYSTEM?

Windows is the operating system that lets you give orders to your computer. The system acts on your commands.

Newer versions of operating systems offer more advantages, so make sure you have the latest version.

There are different versions of Windows for business and home use. Most home users do not need a business version of Windows.

WHAT IS THE DESKTOP?

The Desktop is the working area (background) of the Windows display on your computer.

Look at your desk at home or work. It is the area where you do your paperwork. You pull a file, letter, or your checkbook from a drawer, do some work, and put it back when you are finished. The Desktop of the computer is where you will pull out your electronic files, write electronic letters or work in your computer-based checkbook.

When you start your computer, you will see several screens go by before you arrive at the main Windows screen, which is the Desktop.

WHAT IS THE TASKBAR?

The taskbar is the horizontal bar along the bottom of the Desktop. It has the Start button on the left. Displayed in small rectangles near the middle of the taskbar are the programs that are running. Near the right side, you will see the programs or tasks that start automatically when you start Windows. On the far right, you will see the time displayed.

The taskbar allows you to start your navigation process through all of the computer files.

WHAT IS AN ICON?

An icon is a little picture that represents a program, command or a file.

For instance, the My Computer icon looks like a small computer.

Icons that have a small white arrow in the lower left corner are Shortcuts. The arrow indicates that the icon is a shortcut that points to a program, folder, or other item. A shortcut is a quick way to open a program or file.

WHAT IS A POINTER?

A pointer is the arrow you use to choose things on screen.

Since the Shortcut is simply a pointer to a specific program or file, you can delete the shortcut or remove it from the Desktop without actually deleting the program or file.

WHAT IS THE DIFFERENCE BETWEEN THE (A:), (C:), and (D:) DRIVES?

The (A:) drive is the floppy drive. Older computers used to have two floppy drives, and the second one was the (B:) drive.

The (C:) drive is the hard disk drive. This drive is non-removable.

The (D:) drive is usually the CD-ROM drive. Sometimes it is the (E:) drive.

As more drives are added, they are assigned a letter by the computer.

WHAT IS A FILE?

A file is a collection of information, with a
unique name, stored in your computer or on a
removable disk.

Your checking account could be in one file.
A single letter could be in another file or a
collection of letters could be in one file.

WHAT IS AN EXTENSION?

The last three letters (suffix) of a file name designate an extension. An extension identifies the format of the file. It is preceded by a period.

Every file is in a specific format. There are many different formats. By naming a file with an extension, you tell the computer which format the file is in. That way the computer knows what format to use each time you want to work with that file.

Most programs automatically add the extension suffix when you save your work.

WHAT IS A FOLDER?

Folders are files that can hold multiple documents. They allow you to organize information. Folders can hold both files and other folders (subfolders).

For example, you could put all of your letters to Aunt Mary, in a folder with her name on it; or you could put the Aunt Mary folder into a folder named General Correspondence, that holds many other files and folders.

BOOTING UP

Booting up is a term for starting your personal computer. It initiates an automatic routine that clears the memory, (the computer's, not yours!) loads the operating system, and prepares the computer for use.

To start the computer:

- If this is your first start-up, make a quick check of the cables and plugs to make sure they are all connected.

- Check the floppy-disk drive to be sure it is empty. The computer is looking for instructions to start-up. It will take the instructions from either the floppy drive or the internal hard drive. If a floppy that is not a start-up disk, is in the "A" drive, your PC will display a "non-system disk or disk error" message; and it will not boot up. Relax, it's not a big deal. Just push the eject button and remove the floppy and then press the Spacebar.

- Flip on the surge protector switch, or turn on the computer and monitor power switches. You will hear the machine begin to grumble and grind, and various lights may blink. You'll probably hear a beep. At about the same time you will see some technical messages scrolling by. This is normal. Unless you want to become a propeller head, you do not have to read the technical messages.

WHAT SHOULD I SEE ON THE SCREEN AFTER THE START-UP?

After the start-up, what you should see on the monitor is the Windows Desktop. It is the home base like the physical desk where your computer sits. Several tools to get you started are placed on the background area. These include a taskbar, icons, and a Start button.

There will be variations from computer to computer on what the Desktop looks like.

You will be able to customize the look of your Desktop to suit your artistic feelings!

With Windows XP, the first screen you will see is a "user" choice screen. You can set-up your computer with different settings, themes, choices and passwords, for each user in your household. If you do this, then at START UP the computer will ask you to click on your user name.

WHAT IS A WINDOW?

A window is a framed region on your screen.
It is a rectangular pane with information in it.
Once you have selected an option from a menu,
another window appears. We call that, opening
a window.

RECOGNIZING THE PARTS OF A WINDOW

The window is the rectangular area on the screen. Just like a real window, you can open and close it.

Each window has a title bar at the top. It usually has the program name and the name of the document displayed in it.

The menu bar is located directly under the title bar. It displays a list of command categories. In each category of commands, there are a number of choices.

The toolbar is usually located under the menu bar. It displays a row of buttons for giving commands.

WHAT ARE THE MOUSE FUNCTIONS?

- Pointing. To point to something on the screen, move the mouse over the mouse pad until the pointer is in the spot where you want it. The pointer will move in the same direction that you move the mouse.

- Clicking. Single-clicking is probably the most used mouse function. To click something, point at it and quickly press and release the left mouse button. Do not hold down the button. Generally when you see "click" it refers to a left-click. A right-click is sometimes used to find a shortcut or alternate menu.

- Double-clicking. Point and quickly click the mouse button in rapid succession twice. Double-clicking is also used to initiate action.

- Dragging. To drag, place the mouse pointer where you want to start the drag, press and hold down the mouse button, and then drag the mouse to the ending spot. When you have completed the drag, release the mouse button. Dragging allows you to select text, to move items, and to perform other tasks.

WHAT IS THE TASKBAR?

The taskbar is the bar at the bottom of the Desktop.

Task buttons appear on the taskbar to identify any open applications or programs currently being used.

If a program is minimized (meaning it does not appear on the screen, but is still being used), clicking on it from the taskbar brings it back on-screen. You can easily switch to a different window by clicking its taskbar.

WHAT IS THE START BUTTON?

The Start button is the button that takes you almost anywhere in Windows. It is located on the taskbar. Clicking on the Start button brings up a single menu from which many menus and programs can be accessed.

To display the Start menu, click the Start button. You see the following sub-menus (not necessarily in this order):

Sub-menu	What it does
All Programs	View a list of your programs.
My Documents	Displays your stored documents.
Control Panel	Modify desktop or system settings.
Search	Search for files or folders.
My Pictures	Displays your stored photos.
My Music	Displays your stored music.
My Computer	Displays your stored system and storage devices and allows you access to most files on the computer.

Sub-menu	What it does
My Network Places	Displays the network (if you are connected to a network)
Help and Support	Get answers to your questions.
Run	Open items such as Web pages, programs, and other computer sources.
Log Off	Logs off a specific user of a Windows session.
Turn Off Computer/ Shut Down	Shut down or restart your computer.

The left side of the Start Menu is where you will see your most frequently used programs.

To put a program on your Start button, simply drag any icon from your Desktop onto the Start button.

HOW DO I SHUT DOWN THE PC?

It is important to use the correct shutdown procedure. You should never just shut off your computer.

Before you shut down, always save the files you are working on. Always close Windows before shutting down your computer. This will help to protect your files from data corruption.

To shut down:

- Click the Start button and select Shut Down or Turn Off Computer.

- Select the Shut Down option.

- Click the OK or yes button.

- You will see a screen that tells you it is safe to turn off your PC.

Turn off the power to your computer. Do not forget to turn off the monitor, too.

HOW DO I RESTART THE PC?

Your PC may experience a puzzling failure from time to time. Sometimes it may just freeze up, for no reason at all. DO NOT WORRY. YOU DID NOT DO IT! It is just the nature of computers to get confused on occasion. When this happens your mouse will not respond to clicks and the keyboard stops working. The darn machine does not respond. You may have to restart your computer.

First, try to shutdown the frozen program. Press these three keys at the same time: CTRL, ALT, DEL. Find the program that is not responding, and click End Program.

If that doesn't work, try the menu method. Click the Start button and select Shut Down/Turn Off Computer. Select the Restart Computer button. Click the Yes button.

If that did not work, try the alternate method. Press these two keys at the same time, CTRL and ALT. While holding them down, press DEL three times.

Third, last ditch method, Turn off the power switch.

BASIC SKILLS

Basic skills are used repeatedly in every program. They include selecting text, cutting and pasting text, copying and deleting text. You will also need to know how to open a document, save a document, and print your work.

- Selecting text. Click at the beginning of the text you want to select. Hold down the mouse button and drag across the text. Release the mouse button and the text will appear highlighted.

- Cutting, copying and pasting. These commands are found under the Edit menu. The Cut command allows you to remove text from your document and use it elsewhere. The Copy command lets you duplicate a section of your document, for use elsewhere, without removing it from the original spot. After you have Cut or Copied your selection, move the cursor to the place in the document where you want the section to appear. Then select the Paste option.

- Deleting text. Select the text you want to delete. Press the Delete key. This is different from Cut, as this text is not stored in the computer's memory for your use.

- Saving a document. One of the most important precautions you can take while working is to save your work frequently. On the File menu of the program you are working in, click Save As. The Save As window appears. In the File Name text box there is a blinking cursor or highlighted text. Type in the name you want the file to be called. Click on Save. As you continue working on the same document, you need only to choose the Save command from the File menu.

- Printing your work. From the File menu, choose Print. After making sure all of the options are set as you like them, click on OK.

There is generally a Quick Print icon on the Program menu bar. This will start the printing process. Using this method you will not be able to see the printing options.

OPENING A WINDOW

There are two types of windows, and both types have the same set of controls.

- To open a window displaying the contents of a disk or folder, double-click on the icon. The window is displayed on the Desktop.

- To open a window displaying a program, start the program. The program is started and displayed in a program window.

If you are working in a program, you can have two windows open: the program window and the document window. Each window has its own set of controls. Confusing? Don't worry. With a little practice, you'll be a pro at this.

RESIZING A WINDOW

You may want to change the size of the window to make it easier to read. There are several ways to resize a window.

- Put the pointer on any of the window's borders, but not on the title bar. The mouse pointer turns into a two-headed arrow. Drag the border to change the size of the window.

- Use the Minimize and Maximize buttons that are located in the upper right corner of every window. If you click on the Minimize button, the window disappears. However, you will notice the program button is still on the taskbar. This is different from actually exiting the program that you can do by clicking on the "X" button. This ends or quits the program.

- Instead of quitting the program entirely, minimizing closes only the window of the program. To maximize or open the window again, click on the button on the taskbar.

MOVING A WINDOW

You may want to rearrange where a window is located. Follow these steps to move a window:

- Place the pointer on the window's title bar.

- Drag the title bar to the location you want and release the mouse button.

TOO MANY OPEN WINDOWS?

There are some commands you can use to
"clean up" the window clutter on your Desktop.

- Right-click on the mouse anywhere on the
  taskbar. A menu appears.

- Select Cascade. The Cascade command
  displays the windows so that the title bars of
  each window appear.

- Click on the title bar to bring its window to
  the front of each stack.

- Tile Horizontally stacks each window in
  horizontal panes and Tile Vertically stacks
  each window in vertical panes.

WHAT IS A SCROLL BAR?

A scrollbar is a gray rectangle with small black arrows on both ends. It lets you select the portion of the window you want to see. It is on the right side of a window for vertical scrolling and on the bottom for horizontal scrolling.

When a document is so big it cannot completely be displayed on the monitor, a scroll bar appears so you can see all of its contents by moving the document up and down the screen, or right and left.

The Page Up key scrolls the document up and the Page Down key scrolls it down one full page rather than one line at a time.

By clicking the up/down scroll arrow one time, you will move the document one line at a time.

By clicking on a blank spot above or below the scroll indicator, you will move the document up/down one page. You can continuously scroll by depressing the mouse button steadily instead of by just clicking it.

WHAT IS A MENU?

A menu is a list of commands displayed on your screen, which allows you to perform tasks.

When you click on any of the words in the menu, a list of choices drops down.

Just as you would select your choices from a restaurant menu, you select the choices of what to do on your computer.

WHAT IS A MENU BAR?

A menu bar is an onscreen display that lists available categories of commands. It is usually located at the top of the program window. To choose a category or command, just click on it.

USING MENUS AND SUB-MENUS

It is as simple as this:

- On the menu bar, choose the category of the command that you want. The menu opens.

- Click on the command you want. Voilá!

If a sub-menu opens, it is just giving you more options of how to accomplish your task at hand.

WHAT IS A SHORTCUT MENU?

A shortcut menu, or alternate menu, is a hidden menu that can be opened at any time. Almost every object on your Desktop has one. If you right-click on the item, the shortcut menu will appear.

WHAT ARE THE FUNCTION KEYS?

- **F1-F12.** These are programmable keys called function keys. They provide special functions depending on the software you are using.

- **Esc.** The escape key cancels a command or an operation.

- **Numeric Keypad.** A calculator-style, set of keys for entering numbers.

- **NumLock.** The Number Lock key switches the right-hand keypad between typing numbers and being used as cursor keys.

- **Arrow Keys.** The keys that move the cursor onscreen. The arrow keys move the cursor in the direction indicated by the arrow on each key-one character left or right or one line up or down.

- Page Up (PgUp) and Page Down (PgDn). These keys move the cursor to the preceding screen (PgUp) or the next screen (PgDn).

- Ctrl. The control key pressed in combination with other keys, acts as a shortcut to execute commands and to select commands from the drop down menus.

- Delete (Del). This key deletes the current character.

HOW DO I CLOSE A PROGRAM?

Always remember to close a program when you are finished working in it. Otherwise, it will be taking up memory that other programs may need.

To close a program:

- Save your work.

- Click the Close (x) button in the title bar of the window of the program.

- If you have not saved your work, the program asks you if you want to. Click Yes to save it, click No to lose it.

- The program window disappears.

Alternate method if the close button does not work:

- Go to File.

- Save your work.

- Click Close from the same drop down menu.

WHAT IS A DIALOG BOX?

A dialog box is an onscreen message box or window that enables you to choose options and sends other information to a program. It conveys information to, or requests information from the user.

The computer does its best to do what you want it to do. When it is asked to do something and it needs more information, it starts a dialog with you to see what your intentions are. The dialog box gives you control over how the computer does your tasks.

Sometimes the computer thinks it has enough information to do what you want and goes its merry way. You can always initiate the dialog so that the computer will do what you want it to.

HOW DO I FIND FILES AND FOLDERS?

When you are looking for a particular folder or file, and you are not sure where it is located on your computer, you can use the Find (Search) command instead of opening numerous folders. The Find command lets you quickly search a specific drive or your entire computer. To find a file or folder:

- Click the Start button, point to Find/Search, and then click Files or Folders. The Find dialog box appears.
- In Named, type the file or folder name you want to find.
- Click the Look In down arrow, or click Browse to specify where to search, generally the C: drive.
- Click Find Now. The results of the search will appear.

A word to the wise: start filing your information in an orderly manner at the beginning of your computer experience. It will make life easier. My husband, "bless his heart", never had a filing system in his paper filing cabinet. That same style is reflected in his computer filing. Often, he cannot find his files!

HOW DO I OPEN A FILE OR FOLDER?

After you have located the file you want, you can double-click on it to open it. To find and open a file or folder:

- On the Desktop, double-click My Computer.
- Double-click the drive that contains the file or folder you want to open.
- Double-click the file or folder.

If you have recently opened a file that you want to look at again, check My Documents. You can also open files and folders from the File Open command in the application.

HOW DO I RENAME A FILE OR FOLDER?

It is simple to rename a file or folder. To rename:

- In a window, select the file or folder you want to rename.

- On the File menu, click Rename.

- Type a name and press Enter.

Or

- Select the file or folder you want to rename.

- Right-click on it and select Rename from the shortcut menu.

- Type a name and press Enter.

COPYING AND MOVING FILES AND FOLDERS

When you create files and folders, you may want to copy or move them to another location.

For example, the tax return you just finished is in its own folder named Taxes 2005. You would really like the Taxes 2005 folder to be in the Finances 2005 folder, so you move it to Finances 2005.

To copy or move a file or folder:

- Select the file or folder you want to copy or move. You can select multiple items. To select nonadjacent items, hold down CTRL and click the items you want to select. To select adjacent items, hold down SHIFT while you select items. To select all of the items in a window, on the Edit menu, click Select All.

- On the Edit menu, click Copy (to copy the file) or Cut (to move the file).

- Double-click the folder in which you want to place the file or folder.

- On the Edit menu, click Paste. The file appears in a new location.

Moving program and system files is not recommended.

HOW DO I CREATE A FOLDER?

To create a folder:

- On the Desktop, double-click My Computer. The My Computer window opens.

- Double-click the disk drive or folder in which you want to create a folder. The drive or folder opens.

- On the File menu, point to New, and then click Folder, or an alternate way, right-click a blank area in the window. A new folder appears.

- Type a folder name, and then press Enter. The new folder appears in the location you selected.

DELETING FILES AND FOLDERS

Whenever you delete a file, it is temporarily moved to the Recycle Bin on the Desktop.

If you change your mind, you can restore the file. However, when you empty the Recycle Bin, all of its items are permanently deleted from your computer.

To delete a file:

- Select the file(s) you want to delete, using either My Computer or Windows Explorer.

- Right-click the selected file(s) and then select the Delete command.

- Click Yes when prompted to confirm the deletion.

It is not a good idea to delete program files. If you want to get rid of a program, **Uninstall** it, through the Control Panel and the Add/Remove icon.

HOW DO I CUSTOMIZE MY DESKTOP?

If you don't like the standard color scheme on your Desktop, you can change it. You can use predefined color schemes or make up your own. If your color selections are too wild they may cause eye strain!

To select a background or pattern for the Desktop:

- Right-click on the Desktop.
- Select Properties. The Display Properties dialog box appears. Select Desktop.
- Select Background. Then click Apply and Okay to close the dialog box.

To change any of the screen elements:

- Right-click on the Desktop.
- Select Properties.
- Click on the Appearance tab.
- Display the Scheme drop-down menu and select the color scheme that tickles your fancy.
- Click Apply and Okay to close the dialog box.

HOW DO I PLAY A CD?

Playing music with the CD Player is very simple. A feature called auto-play detects when you insert a CD into the CD-ROM drive and automatically starts the music for you.

If auto-play does not work, here is how to do it manually. Follow these steps to play a CD:

- Click the Start button.
- Select All Programs.
- Select Accessories.
- Select Entertainment.
- Select Windows Media Player.
- Insert a disk into the CD drive.
- Click Play.

PLAYING SOUNDS

Most sounds are stored in WAV (wave) files. To play a sound:

- Click the Start button.
- Select All Programs.
- Select Accessories.
- Select Entertainment.
- Select Sound Recorder.
- From the Sound Recorder window open the File menu.
- Select Open. In the Open dialog box that appears, change to the drive and folder that contains the file you want to play.
- When you see the sound file you want to play, double-click on it.
- To play the sound, click the Play button.

SOUND RECORDER TOOLBAR

The control buttons look much like the buttons on a typical voice recorder, and they work in much the same way.

- Seek to Start (double, left pointing triangles).
  Rewinds to beginning of sound file.
- Seek to End (double, right pointing triangles).
  Fast forward to the end of the sound file.
- Play (single, right pointing triangle).
  Plays the sound.
- Stop (big rectangle).
  Stops the playback.
- Record (big red circle).
  Records the new sound.

PLAYING MEDIA CLIPS AND MOVIES

To play a media file (AVI, WAV, or MID and RMI):

- Click the Start button.
- Select Programs.
- Select Accessories.
- Select Entertainment.
- Select Media Player. Windows will display the Media Player program.
- Open the File menu.
- Select Open.
- When you see the file you want to play, double-click it.
- To play the clip, click the Play button.

WHAT IS A SCREEN SAVER?

A screen saver is a program that displays an image or animation on your screen when your PC is idle.

It was invented to insure that all parts of the monitor screen received equal amounts of illumination so a ghost image would not be "burned" onto the screen. Today's monitors don't have burn-in problems.

Screen savers are fun and often entertaining. You can use any number of pre-installed screensavers or you can use screensavers downloaded from the internet. You can even use any of your saved digital photos.

HOW DO I GET A SCREEN SAVER?

Windows comes with many screen savers as part of the package. There are many more screen savers available commercially. To find the screen savers included with Windows:

- Right-click on a blank spot on the Desktop, and choose Properties to open the Display Properties dialog box.
- On the Screen Saver tab, select an option from the drop-down list.
- Click OK to make this your screen saver.

To use images you have stored on your computer as your screen saver:

- Right-click on Desktop.
- Select Screen Saver tab.
- Highlight My Pictures slide show.
- Click Apply and Okay to close the dialog box.

WHAT IS A PROGRAM?

Program is synonymous with software. It is a set of instructions, written in programming language, that a computer can execute, to perform your tasks in a certain way.

WINDOWS PROGRAMS

Windows comes with four types of programs:

- Accessory programs. Located in the Accessories folder in the Program menu. They include: Accessibility, Communications, Entertainment, Games, System Tools, Calculator, Imaging, Keyboard Manager, Notepad, Paint and WordPad.

- Control Panel programs. The control panel allows you to adjust how all of the pieces/parts of your computer work. You will find these programs by clicking The Start button and then selecting Control Panel.

- Preloaded Software that may include word processing, financial management or digital imagery.

- MS-DOS prompt. MS-DOS refers to typed code used to make the computer do its work. Windows uses a graphical representation of the MS-DOS code, which is a great improvement in user friendliness. Do not worry about this function. It is rarely used these days.

NEW PROGRAMS

The more you work with your computer, the more you can do with it. Eventually, you will probably think to yourself, "I'll bet there is a specialized program to help me do this task." You bet there is! You can find programs that will do just about anything.

However, before you buy a new program, make sure that you can run that program on your system. Check the system requirements (usually printed on the side of the software box). These include type of microprocessor, amount of memory, hard disk space, video card, and any other required equipment.

Today, most software ships on CD or DVD discs. Some software still ships on 3.5 inch diskettes. You must have the appropriate drive for the particular media you buy.

You need to install the new software from the disc or diskettes onto your system. Most software applications include instructions for installing the software. On the next page, I have included some basic steps for installing new software in Windows. If the instructions included with the software differ greatly from these, I recommend you use the instructions included with the software.

Software can also be purchased and downloaded via the internet. No need to go to the store! Simply follow the instructions from the vendor's web site.

Warning! Make sure you know who you are downloading from before you purchase a program.

HOW DO I ADD A NEW PROGRAM?

To add a program:

- Insert the installation disk in the drive. If you are installing from a disc that has an AutoRun feature, when you insert the disc, the installation program starts automatically.

If the installation prompt doesn't come up automatically:

- Click the Start button, select Settings, and select Control Panel. Double-click Add/Remove programs.
- Click Install button.
- Click the Finish button
- Follow the on-screen instructions.

You can also use the Run Command to install a program. To use the Run Command:

- Insert the program disk into the drive. Click the Start button.

HOW DO I ADD A NEW PROGRAM, CONT.

- Select Run. The Run dialog box appears.
- Type the drive letter (ex. C:\).
- Click the OK button.
- Click the Installer (disc) icon.

Follow the on-screen instructions for installing the program.

If you have downloaded a program from the internet, find the icon for it on your Desktop and click it. A dialog box will open and guide you through the process.

HOW DO I REMOVE A PROGRAM?

The best way to uninstall a program is by using the Add/Remove Program icon, located in the Control Panel.

It is not a good idea to simply delete the program folder. The original program installation may have put files in other folders and changed some of the system settings.

To remove a program:

- Click the Start button.
- Select Control Panel. You see the program icons in the Control Panel.
- Double-click the Add/Remove icon.
- If necessary, click the Install/Uninstall button.
- Select the program you want to uninstall.
- Click the Add/Remove button.

HOW DO I START A PROGRAM?

Most of the programs installed on your computer are available from the Programs section of the Start menu. To start a program:

- Click the Start button.
- Click All Programs. The Program menu appears.
- Click on the program name that contains the program you want to start.

If the program is stored in a folder, point to the folder. Do this until you see the program icon. Then click the icon to start the program.

HOW DO I QUIT A PROGRAM?

To quit a program:

- Click the Close button in the upper-right corner of the program window.

Or

- From the File menu, click Close.

WORD PROCESSING OVERVIEW

A word processor is a program that enables you to create documents that you might have once created with a typewriter. You can create letters, memos, reports, lists, invitations, and much, much more.

To make the job easier, most word processors offer grammar and spell checking tools. Some include built-in reference works such as synonym finders and almanacs.

The most popular word processors are Microsoft Word and WordPerfect.

SPREADSHEET OVERVIEW

A spreadsheet program lets you create electronic ledgers in which calculations are done instantly and automatically. Spreadsheet programs can translate your data into charts and graphs.

The most popular spreadsheet programs are Microsoft Excel and Lotus 1-2-3.

GAMES

There are many games available for your PC. If there is a game you have been playing for years, chances are it has been created in an electronic format. Chess, bridge, solitaire, and more games exist for your entertainment.

Windows comes with a few games. They are located in the Accessories, Games directory.

WHAT IS MULTITASKING?

Multitasking means that your computer can execute more than one program at a time. You can have more than one window open at a time.

For example, you are able to write using your word processing program while your spreadsheet program prints a report.

WHAT IS THE MY COMPUTER DIRECTORY?

The My Computer icon represents one way to see everything on your system. It allows you to browse drives, directories (folders), and files in separate ways.

An icon that looks like a folder represents each directory.

To use My Computer to view the hard disk:

- On the Desktop, double-click My Computer. The My Computer window appears.
- Double-click the icon that represents your hard disk. Your hard disk window appears, and the contents of your hard disk appear.

USING WINDOWS EXPLORER

Another way to see everything in your system is with Windows Explorer. Instead of opening drives and folders in separate windows, you can browse through them in a single window, in a hierarchical structure.

The left side of the Windows Explorer window contains a list of your drives and folders, and the right side displays the contents of the selected folder. You can use View menu to change how the icons in the right half of the window appear.

To use Windows Explorer to view the hard disk:

- Click the Start button.
- Select All Programs. Click on Accessories.
- Click on Windows Explorer.
- In the left pane, click the letter that represents your hard disk.
- The contents of your hard disk appear in the right pane.

WORKING WITH MY DOCUMENTS

The My Documents folder on the Desktop is a convenient place for you to store frequently used files and folders.

For easy access to a file that you use frequently, you can also create a shortcut to it. A shortcut does not change the location of the file. The shortcut is just a pointer that lets you open the file quickly.

To open recently used documents click on the Start button, and then point to My Documents. A list of your documents appears. Click on a document in the list and the document opens. To move a file to the My Documents folder, drag the file to the My Documents folder on your Desktop.

To create a shortcut to a file, use the right mouse button to drag the file to the Desktop. On the menu that appears, click Create Shortcut(s). The shortcut appears on the Desktop. You can copy or move the shortcut to another location.

FILE MANAGEMENT

File management is just that, managing or organizing your directories and files to make your computer as efficient as possible.

Much like a filing cabinet has file folders, a hard disk can be divided into folders. You can store like files together in a folder.

A folder can contain files or other folders.

BACKING UP

Backing up means creating a copy of all the files on your system, to another drive.

It is very important to periodically backup all of the data files on your computer. If something happens to your computer you can always reinstall them from a copy.

If something happens to your data and you do not have a backup copy, you are in a pickle. How often you backup depends on how important the data is to you.

There are several ways to store your back up copy. You can back up to floppy disks, to another hard drive, to a special tape backup drive, to a CD-RW, or to a completely separate backup system such as a large, removable storage device.

Be sure to put your backup copies in a safe place away from your computer. In case of a disaster, you will want your backup copies in a secure location.

HARD DISK MAINTENANCE

Over time, hard drives slow down, due to storing files in separate clusters. This is normal.

To keep your system running in tiptop condition, you should regularly give your hard drive a tune-up.

By using Scan Disk/Error Checking and Defragment, you will keep your computer running efficiently.

Computers store information in clusters. However, the clusters of one file may not all be stored in the same area of the hard drive. When this happens, the disk is "fragmented". The computer has to go to several places in the storage space to get it and reassemble it for you. To improve the performance, you can straighten up the disk and put files back in order.

To defragment your hard drive:

- Back up your system before you start defragmenting.
- Double-click the My Computer icon.
- Right-click the disk you want to check.
- Select Properties.

- Click the Tools tab.
- Click Defragment now.
- Click the Start button. Windows displays the progress on screen.
- When the defragmentation is complete and you are prompted to defragment another drive, click the No button.

Scan Disk/Error Checking checks for and fixes damage to the drive. To run Scan Disk/Error Checking:

- Double-click the My Computer icon.
- Right-click the disk you want to check.
- Select Properties.
- Click the Tools tab.
- Click the Check Now button. Windows displays two Check Disk options. Check both boxes.
- Click the Start button. Windows checks your drive and if it finds any errors, it will display a dialog that explains the error and your options.
- Select a correction method. Click OK.
- Review this info and then click Close.

If Windows wants to do the work the next you restart your computer, say yes.

WHAT IS THE INTERNET?

The Internet is a worldwide network of computers. The computers "talk" to each other electronically, relaying information and sharing common links that allow you to gather information from around the world.

The computers that make up the Internet are known as servers. Their job is to store data (information, pictures, etc.) and "serve" them upon request, to computers known as clients.

The Internet is often referred to as the "Net". The word Internet is a contraction of international and network.

WHERE DID THE INTERNET ORIGINATE?

The Internet was the invention of the Advanced Research Projects Agency of the U.S. Department of Defense. It was developed in the 60's as a way for scientists and government officials to communicate in the event of a nuclear war. It was called ARPANET.

WHAT IS THE WORLD WIDE WEB?

The World Wide Web is a system for accessing information on the Internet. It is the graphical, multimedia portion of the Internet.

The Web links one Internet site to another with hypertext links. With hypertext links, you click on words that are highlighted in a passage and jump to a new location where more information on that subject is provided.

Do not expect every resource on the Internet to be accessible through the Web. To be accessible, a document must be coded with links that can be read by Web servers.

E-mail and newsgroups are not part of the Web.

WHAT CAN I DO ON THE INTERNET?

There are plenty of things you can do on the Internet.

- You can find information on anything from A to Z.
- You have access to huge databases, libraries, and museums.
- You can send and receive e-mail.
- You can shop online.
- You can participate in online discussions.
- You can download files from a site to your PC.
- You can make money on the Internet.
- You can even create your own web page, a place where people can learn about you.

To learn about the author, go to:
www.theseniorsguide.com

WHO OWNS AND RUNS THE INTERNET?

The Internet consists of a Federally funded network tied to thousands of sub-networks. No government controls the Internet and there is no central administrator or owner.

The networks share a common set of standards for addressing and transmitting messages, but the contents and information are wholly unregulated. No one verifies the accuracy of the information or censors the available information.

HOW MANY PEOPLE ARE ON THE INTERNET?

This number changes daily. The International Data Corporation estimates worldwide users of the Internet numbered 38 million in 1994, 56 million in 1995, and 256 million in 1999. Today there are over 605 million internet users. In 2007 it is estimated there will be over one billion internet users worldwide.

IS THERE BAD STUFF ON THE INTERNET?

The Internet is just like anywhere else. There is information that everyone is happy to see and information that you never want to see. There are more safe sites than unsafe sites.

The Internet allows people to meet without face to face contact. Wherever people congregate, there always seem to be a few bad apples in the barrel.

It is possible to block access to certain sites which are inappropriate for children. Most ISPs can block the bad stuff at the server level. Internet Explorer features the PICS (Platform for Internet Content Selection) system. It allows you to set ratings for language, nudity, sex, and violence. Check the Options menu under Content settings.

SECURITY ON THE INTERNET

Always make sure your transactions are done over a secure server. A secure server encrypts your information. That means that the information has been scrambled by software to make it unreadable by anyone but the receiving computer.

Web browsers Internet Explorer and Netscape Navigator include security features that let you know when your connection is secure and when it is not. A secure site is denoted with a locked padlock in the bottom bar of the browser window.

Be careful out there. Keep in mind that digital information is easily manipulated. Do not give out any information unless you know the receiver. Be a smart shopper.

Never give out your passwords to anyone over the Internet.

WHAT DO I NEED TO GET ONLINE?

Welcome to cyberspace! To get online, you will
need:

- A computer.

- A modem.

- A telephone line connection, cable
  connection or satellite dish.

- And an Internet Service Provider (ISP) and
  their access software.

HOW DO I GET CONNECTED?

The most popular way to connect is by using a modem and dialing up through the standard telephone network. This is the cheapest, but slowest way to connect.

A second phone line, dedicated for computer use, can be very beneficial. On the home front, this means that you can still receive telephone calls while you are online.

The better options are cable, DSL or satellite access. They will offer extreme speed rates for a fixed monthly charge. Call your local cable TV operator/DSL provider/Satellite dish provider to find out if it is available in your area.

WHAT IS AN ISP?

ISP stands for Internet Service Provider. It is an entity that has the communications and computer facilities that let you connect to its Internet link. Usually there is a fee for this service.

Sometimes the ISP is referred to as the host or server. A server makes files available to other computers. The client (your computer) uses software so you can perform online functions.

There are many ISPs from which to choose. There are local, national, and international providers. The local providers are usually independent and may limit their services to Internet access and e-mail. National and international providers offer not only Internet access and e-mail, but also many members-only services and content. When looking for a provider, consider if they provide easy access to resources, services and information that is of the greatest interest to you. All providers are not equal.

WHICH ONLINE SERVICE IS THE BEST?

These days there are many excellent online providers available. Some of the most popular are: AOL, Compuserve, Microsoft Network, Earthlink, Comcast, Dish, Direct TV, Starband.

CAN I SWITCH ONLINE SERVICES?

Sure, no problem. You can cancel at any time.
Canceling one service does not mean you
cannot try another. In fact, you can subscribe to
more than one service at a time. Just remember
that you will be billed for each service.

WHERE DO I GET THE SOFTWARE TO ACCESS THE INTERNET?

Usually your ISP provides the necessary software. If your provider does not provide free software, maybe they are not the best provider choice.

WHAT IS A WEB BROWSER?

A Web browser is the key piece of Internet software needed to access and navigate the Web. The interface enables you to ask for and view Web pages.

Browsers vary in quality and in the number of accessories they offer. They also take up a lot of disk space.

Two of the most popular browsers are Internet Explorer and Netscape Navigator.

If you have Windows on your computer, you already have Internet Explorer.

HOW TO CHOOSE A BROWSER

Most Internet Service Providers supply a browser as part of the start-up software. It is likely to be Internet Explorer. There was a time when Netscape was not free of charge so most providers went with Internet Explorer, which was free.

Both Internet Explorer and Netscape Navigator are highly capable and easy to use. Both have their strengths. Although each Web browser is different, they all use the same basic processes. Ultimately it comes down to a matter of personal preference.

WHAT IS A DOMAIN NAME?

A domain name identifies and locates a host computer or service on the Internet. It is the identifying title given to a system of computers. It is registered in much the same way as a company name.

Currently, domain types are usually one of the following:

.com   Company or commercial organization.

.edu   Educational institution.

.gov   Government body.

.mil   Military site.

.net   Internet gateway or administrative host.

.org   Non-profit organization.

HOW DO I LOG ON TO THE INTERNET?

You are ready to log on if you have a computer with a modem, an Internet browser, and an ISP.

There are many ways to set up a PC Internet connection due to different operating systems, PC configurations, and Web browsers. Follow the instructions for installing the connection software. Then follow the instructions for logging on to the Internet. It will be something like this:

- Double-click the Internet icon. The installation program sets up an icon for Internet access.

- When prompted, sign on. For most Internet connections, you type your user name and password.

- When you connect, you will see your home page.

WHAT IS A WEB PAGE/WEB SITE?

A Web page is a document on the Web. Web pages can include text, pictures, and sound. They also can contain links that connect you to other Web pages.

Different locations on the Web are known as Web sites. A Web site is comprised of one or more Web pages.

WHAT IS A HOME PAGE?

The first page of a Web site is often called a home page. It is the primary Web page for an individual, software application, or organization.

Home page also has another meaning. It refers to the page that appears when you start your browser and acts as your home base for exploring the Web.

WHAT IS HYPERTEXT AND LINKING?

Web pages are written in HTML (HyperText Markup Language). They contain hyperlink connections to other documents. These connections are embedded within the text.

A hyperlink is a connector between the Web page you are currently viewing and another, somewhere else. It is a signpost to take you to other Web pages with related information. It appears as an icon, graphic, or word in a file, that when clicked with the mouse, automatically opens another file for viewing.

A link is usually underlined or displayed in a different color. If the link happens to be an image, the mouse pointer turns into a "hand" to show that the image is a link.

To pursue a link, click on the highlighted text or image. You will be able to jump to the new site.

WHAT IS A URL?

Each Web page has a unique address called a URL: uniform resource locator. It is a standardized addressing system for material accessible over the Internet. Most Web pages include text, graphics, and links to other Web pages. These unique individual addresses allow you to go to specific web sites and pages.

If you know a site's URL, you can go directly to it by entering the URL in the address field and pressing Enter.

Each URL has three parts: the protocol, the host name, and the file path.

The "http" part that appears at the beginning identifies the document as a Web page. The remainder of the URL, reading from left to right identifies the domain and any sub-domains within the site. The slashes are dividers that are necessary for the address.

Example:
http://www.thseniorsguide.com

WHAT IS THE MEANING OF http?

http stands for hypertext transfer protocol and refers to set a rules used by your browser to access and display the page.

Don't worry, this is not a set of rules you have to learn!

HOW TO SURF THE WEB

You can browse or surf the Web in several ways.

- You can open any Web page by typing its address in the Address box of your Web browsing software.

- When you are viewing a Web page, you can surf to related sites by clicking the links on the page.

- You can also use toolbar buttons to move between Web pages, search the Internet, or to refresh a Web page's content.

INTERNET EXPLORER TOOLBAR BUTTONS

Back   Moves to a previously viewed Web page.

Forward   Moves to the next Web page.

Stop   Stops the downloading of a Web page.

Refresh   Updates the currently displayed Web page.

Home   Jumps to your home page.

Search   Opens a Web page that lists the available search engines.

Favorites   Displays a list of Web pages you have designated as your favorites.

History   Displays a list of recently visited sites.

Channels   Displays a list of channels you can select.

Fullscreen Uses a smaller Standard toolbar and hides the Address bar so more of the screen is visible.

Mail Opens Outlook Express or Internet News.

Print Prints a Web page.

Edit Opens FrontPage Express so you can edit a Web page.

HOW DO I SEARCH FOR A TOPIC?

To search the Web you use a search engine. A search engine is a program that allows you to locate specified information from a database.

It looks like a normal Web page, with a form to enter the search terms that you are looking for. Type the word or phrase you want to find and click the Search button. The search engine then displays the matches.

The various search engines source, store, and retrieve their data differently. My favorite is Google. Others include HotBot, AltaVista, Yahoo, Infoseek, Excite, DogPile.

The computer can do quite a bit for you, but it does not know your intentions. For example, if you put Levi's in the search parameter, hoping to find a new pair of blue jeans, don't be surprised if you get an essay on the history of indigo ink. The search engine looks for the keyword that you typed. If it is in the document, it will display it.

CANNOT OPEN A WEB PAGE?

It is just a matter of time before you click on a link or Web address that does not work. There are a couple of reasons this might happen.

If only one URL does not work, you know that it is either a wrong address or the host at its end has problems. Web addresses can change because their addresses have been simplified. Addresses must be exact or you will not get to the site that you are looking for.

If none of the URLs work, check to make sure you have an Internet connection. If you cannot connect to any Web site, close and reopen your browser. You might be having a software glitch or a connection problem.

Often your browser will pop-up with a message and error code pointing the way to solving the problem.

WEB ADDRESS ERROR CODES

- Incorrect host name. When the address points to a nonexistent host, your browser will return an error saying, "Host not found".

- Illegal domain name. The illegal host name is more than likely from keying in an address with the wrong punctuation, a single slash instead of two slashes, or forgetting to put a dot after www.

- File not found. If the file has moved, changed names, or you have overlooked capitalization, you will get a message from the server telling you the file does not exist on the host.

- Host refuses entry. The host is either overloaded with traffic or temporarily off-limits and may not let you gain entry.

WHAT IS AN FTP PROGRAM?

FTP stands for File Transfer Protocol. It is the standard way to transfer files between computers. Before you can download anything, you will need an FTP program. The browsers, Netscape and Internet Explorer, include a file transfer program.

Whew! I bet you thought you would have to go shopping for one.

HOW DO I DOWNLOAD A FILE FROM THE WEB?

When you download a file, you are retrieving information you want from an online service, onto your own computer.

When you download a file, the online service sends you a copy of the file. To retrieve it, click on the link and follow the prompts. Before sending the file to you, it asks you where on your hard drive you want to store the file and what you want to name the file.

Always look at how big the file is that you are expecting to download. You need to make sure that you have enough space on your computer to hold it. Also, take in to consideration how much time it will take to download. You probably do not want to have your telephone tied up for hours if you are expecting a call.

Organize your downloads (which are just files coming from another computer) just like the files you already have on your computer.

WHAT IS UPLOADING?
WHAT IS DOWNLOADING?

If you send a file to another computer, you upload the file.

If you receive a file from another computer, you download it.

IS THERE AN EASY WAY TO RETURN TO MY FAVORITE SPOTS?

You can mark the location of your favorite Web sites. Internet Explorer calls it adding to your "Favorites". Netscape calls it adding to your "Bookmarks".

When you find a site that you like and want to come back to, click the Favorites menu, and then click, Add To Favorites. You can now go back there with a click of the mouse. You can do the same thing in Netscape, under Bookmarks.

WHAT IS A NEWSGROUP?

A newsgroup is an online discussion or forum group, dealing with a wide range of topics. It is an electronic bulletin board of messages. People from all over the world can respond to other people's messages. You can even start new discussions.

Each newsgroup is focused on a particular topic. Usenet consists of over 25,000 newsgroups.

To access and review newsgroup postings, you need a newsreader. This program is included in Internet Explorer and Netscape Communicator.

Once again, a sigh of relief. You don't have to buy this separately!

WHAT ARE CHAT ROOMS?

Chat rooms are the equivalent of meeting rooms in which you can carry on live keyboard conversations with everyone in the room as a group or with particular individuals.

Chats take place in a chat room, a forum, or via an Internet Relay Channel (IRC). There are two basic kinds of chats: Web based and IRC. Most Web based chat rooms are easier to access and are devoted to general subject matter.

Do you remember your mother telling you not to talk to strangers? Well, unless you already know the people in a chat room, they are all strangers. Be careful. Be smart about the information you exchange.

WHAT IS A PLUG-IN?

A plug-in is an auxiliary program that works alongside your browser. It is a script, utility, or a set of instructions that add to the functionality of a program without changing the program's base code. You download it, install it, and your browser will call on it only when it needs it.

Two great plug-ins, are RealPlayer and Shockwave. RealPlayer is for Internet music and video broadcasts and Shockwave is for multimedia effects.

They are included with Internet Explorer.

WHAT IS A COOKIE?

A cookie is information from a Web site sent to a browser and stored on your hard drive so the Web site can retrieve it later. It is like an ID card. The next time you drop by the site, it will actually know your individual browser.

Most Web sites routinely log your visit. The cookie contains information that is recorded against your IP (Internet Protocol) address. However, many dial-up users are issued a different IP address each time they log on.

You have the option to configure your browser to either accept or reject cookies.

Some sites require your computer to accept cookies. If you need to go to that site, you have to accept their cookies.

WHAT IS A VIRUS?

A virus is an unwanted file or set of instructions that attaches itself to files in your computer system, usually causing harm to your computer. It replicates itself as the file is shared from computer to computer.

Viruses are not naturally occurring bugs. People, who want to damage your computer system, create them.

You can protect yourself from viruses by always checking programs and files that you download from the Internet with a virus protection program. You can purchase protection programs from a computer store. The two most popular programs are McAfee's Anti Virus and Norton's AntiVirus.

Even people you know and trust can accidentally send you a virus, so you really should use your virus protection program regularly.

If your anti-virus program has an automatic e-mail protection system, use it.

LOGGING OFF THE INTERNET

To log off:

Exit your browser by

- Clicking the Close button on your browser.

or

- Look for a Sign Off command or Disconnect button.

If you are using a telephone dial-up modem, you may need to terminate the call manually, depending on how your program is set up.

WHAT IS E-MAIL?

E-mail is short for electronic mail. It is digital correspondence.

E-mail gives you the ability to send and receive text messages to/from anyone with an e-mail address. You can attach other files, pictures, or programs to your message.

E-mail is more like a conversation than a formal correspondence. It is a speedy way to get a message to someone. It should be concise and to the point, as well as, well written. Do not forget to check your spelling and grammar and punctuation. Your teachers were right. Spelling counts!

E-mail is fast. It is easy. It is inexpensive.

HOW DOES E-MAIL WORK?

When someone sends you a message, that message is sent to your Internet Service Provider, and stored there. When you log on and check your e-mail, the message is sent from the server to your computer.

WHAT DO I NEED TO GET STARTED?

- You need to be able to go online.
- You have to connect your modem to a telephone line, DSL line, cable TV or Satellite dish.
- You must have an account with an Internet Service Provider.
- You will also need an e-mail software program (usually provided by your ISP or included in the Web browser).
- You have to have an e-mail address.

The two most popular e-mail programs are Internet Explorer's Outlook Express and Netscape's Messenger.

You automatically get an e-mail address when you sign up with an ISP or online service, such as AOL, or Compuserve.

Setting up is simple. The exact steps you follow to send and receive mail, will vary from program to program. However, the e-mail options are always prominently displayed on the Menu screen and in their own pull-down menu.

WHAT'S IN AN E-MAIL ADDRESS?

The Internet Service Provider assigns an e-mail address to you. Usually you can choose your user name.

The first part of the address (before the @) is a user name. The second part, or domain name, defines the Internet provider where the mail is sent. The two parts are separated by an @ sign (pronounced "at").

The domain name is followed by an extension that indicates the type of organization to which the network belongs.

Here is an example of an address:
rscolmer@theseniorsguide.com

HOW DO I SEND E-MAIL?

To send mail:

- Start your e-mail program.
- Click the Compose New Message option. Depending on your e-mail program, the name of this button may vary.
- In the To box, type the address of the recipient or click on a name in the address book.
- Type a short description of your e-mail on the Subject line.
- Click the message area and type your message.
- To send the message, click the Send button.

Most people compose all of their e-mail messages offline. This saves connection time that you buy from your ISP. Before you can actually send the message, you need to go online.

HOW CAN I BE SURE THAT MY MESSAGE WAS SENT?

If you are not sure if you really sent a message, there is a way to find out.

Look through your icons or menu choices for the Out Box. In some mail programs, when you open that box, you will see some indication that your message has been sent.

In most mail programs the message is marked with a check mark.

There may also be a Sent Message file in your filing cabinet that you can check. Outlook Express takes messages from the Out Box, sends them, and files a copy in the Sent Message file.

HOW DO I RECEIVE AND READ MAIL?

To check for new mail:

- Be online.
- Start your e-mail program.
- Check for new messages. When new mail arrives, you will hear a sound, get a message and/or see a little envelope in your system tray.
- Your mail program collects all the messages on your mail server and displays them in your In Box.
- To read a message, double-click it.

Most people read all of their mail offline. This saves connection time.

Once you have read a message, your e-mail program will give you choices for handling the message. You can read and close the message, or you can choose to print the message. You can also reply to the sender, reply to everyone listed in the header, or send it to someone else. Or you can delete the message.

HOW DO I USE THE ADDRESS BOOK?

Most mail programs allow you to store frequently used addresses in an address book. There is no need to memorize each address. You do not even have to type in the whole address each time.

Start your address book by putting in your own address.

In Outlook Express:

- Open Tools menu.
- Choose Address Book.
- Choose New Contact and fill in the blanks.

You can manually enter each name and e-mail address by opening the address book and entering the information or if you receive e-mail from someone simply right-click on the sender's name and choose "Add to Address Book".

ADDRESSING E-MAIL SHORTCUT

After you have a person's e-mail address in your address book, you can simply open your address book and double-click on the name of your choosing. The program will bring up a screen for you to compose e-mail to that person. What a time saver!

HOW DO I REPLY TO E-MAIL?

To reply to an e-mail message:

- Click on the piece of mail to open it.

- Click on the Reply button. This will automatically copy the original message and address it back to the sender.

- Type your message.

- Click the Send button.

HOW DO I FORWARD E-MAIL?

To forward e-mail:

- Click the Forward button.

- In the To Box, type the address of that person.

- Click the Send button.

SENDING CARBON COPIES AND BLIND CARBON COPIES

If you want to send two or more people the same message, and you do not mind if they know whom else is receiving it:

- Type one address in the To box.
- Type the other addresses in the CC (carbon copy) field.

To send a mailing without disclosing the list of recipients, put yourself in the To box, and everyone else in BCC (blind carbon copy).

If you put recipients into the BCC field, their names and addresses are masked from all others. However, everyone, including those in BCC can see who's in To and CC.

HOW DO I ATTACH A FILE TO MY E-MAIL MESSAGE?

To send a file, like a word processing document, spreadsheet, or an image:

- Look in the mail menu for Attach File or Send Attachments. Or, look for a "paper clip" icon on the toolbar.

- You will be prompted for the file name and its location on your hard drive.

- Once you navigate to the file, double-click on it. A copy of it will be attached to your e-mail. When you actually send your e-mail, the attached file will be sent right along with it.

HOW DO I RECEIVE ATTACHMENTS?

When someone sends you an e-mail with an attachment, you will generally see it as an icon at the bottom of your e-mail, with a name next to it. In most cases, you can just double-click on the icon.

Do not open an attachment if you do not know who sent it to you. Some attachments can contain viruses that can harm your hard disk.

As an example, my husband recently received an e-mail from an acquaintance. The e-mail included a greeting card titled "Happy99.exe". When he opened it, it was a fireworks animation. Very pretty. It was a virus. This particular virus hid in his computer and sent itself to people on his e-mail list without his knowledge.

Once again, an anti-virus program with an automatic e-mail checker is a great tool.

IS E-MAIL PRIVATE?

No. E-mail is never confidential. Without encryption, the possibility exists that e-mail can be accessed and read by others.

Your recipient can forward it to others.

Do not send anything that you would not mind reading about on the front page of your local newspaper.

It is a good practice to log onto the Internet, retrieve your mail, and then log off. Your mail is available for you to read when you are offline.

You may also respond to your mail or write new mail while you are offline. Then log on to send your e-mail.

EMOTICONS

Smiley's typically appear at the end of a sentence to reinforce what was just said. Here are a few:

- Smile   :-)

- Also a smile   :)

- Grin   :-}

- Laughing   :-D

- Smirk   :-1

- Frown   :-(

- Undecided   :-\

- Mad   >:-<

(Turn your head sideways if the punctuation above just looks like punctuation. Now you've got it!)

E-MAIL ETIQUETTE

Another name for e-mail etiquette is netiquette. While online you should practice all of the social rules of good behavior. Because you will often be communicating with people whom you have never met, you should follow some basic rules.

- No shouting. Typing in all upper case letters signifies shouting online.

- No flaming. When another online person posts an opinion that you think is outrageous or ridiculous, do not be tempted to respond with excessive outrage. Keep your language and temper under control.

- No spamming. Do not post the same message to hundreds of newsgroups. Most recipients do not appreciate this sort of advertising.

- Save your humor for your good friends. It can easily be misinterpreted.

ACRONYMS

Here are some commonplace, shorthand expressions:

- AFAIK   As far as I know.
- BRB   Be right back.
- BTW   By the way.
- IMHO   In my humble opinion.
- EOL   End of lecture.
- RSN   Real soon now.
- TIA   Thanks in advance.
- LOL   Laughing out loud.
- GMTA   Great minds think alike.
- TTFN   Ta ta for now.
- WYSIWYG   What you see is what you get.
- IANALB   I am not a lawyer, but.
- FWIW   For what it's worth.
- ROTFL   Rolling on the floor laughing.
- SOHF   Sense of human failure.
- IDK   I don't know.

1. Check out my web site on a frequent basis, www.theseniorsguide.com

2. Consider getting an additional telephone line if you are on the Internet a lot. Consider moving up to DSL, cable or satellite.

3. Pressing F1 opens Help information in most programs.

4. Whenever you see "Press Any Key", remember that you can press any key you choose: x, y, and z, the Spacebar, whatever you like. There is not an "any" key.

5. Press Ctrl, Alt, Del simultaneously to send Windows a signal to shut down. You can use this combination to quit a program that is freezing up.

6. You can select a group of files by selecting the first one and then holding down the Ctrl key while you select the others.

7. A good way to practice using the mouse is to play Solitaire. You will get the feel of the mouse by clicking and dragging.

8. If you are formatting an existing disk, be sure the disk does not contain any information that you need. Formatting erases all of the information on the disk.

9. To avoid problems, close all open programs before starting any program installation.

10. A zip drive is a type of disk with a higher density than a floppy disk. You can store more information on it than on a floppy disk.

11. To rename a shortcut icon, simply right-click the icon, select Rename, and type in a new name. Press Enter.

12. Perform regular housekeeping and delete those files that are no longer needed.

13. A "local" access number may still be a toll call. Check with your operator to be sure that it is a local call.

14. If you subscribe to an online mailing list, be sure you know how to un-subscribe.

15. Macintosh and PC users can send e-mail to each other.

16. Always spell check your documents. Spell checkers will catch spelling errors, duplication errors, and most typical non-spelling errors.

17. When you buy software, be sure to send in the registration card. The company will then keep you posted about upgrades and future releases.

18. When describing a CD, the term "disc" is used instead of "disk". They are pronounced the same.

19. Some games are DOS programs and are installed and run from MS-DOS mode. If you need to install a DOS game or program, you can restart your PC in MS-DOS mode by selecting Restart in MS-DOS mode.

20. If you want to see Calculator's scientific side, click View at the top of the Calculator window, and then click Scientific. To turn it back to the original, click View again and then click Standard.

21. Reshaping or resizing a window is an easy way to get rid of scroll bars. Just keep stretching the window until the scroll bar you do not want, goes away. No matter how hard you try, some windows cannot let you see all of the contents at one time.

22. Using keyboard shortcuts, instead of the mouse and drop-down menus, can make your work go faster.

23. The keyboard shortcut for Display Properties Box is ALT-ENTER.

24. The keyboard shortcut for Bold is CTRL-B.

25. The keyboard shortcut for Italics is CTRL-I.

26. The keyboard shortcut for Underline is CTRL-U.

27. The keyboard shortcut for Cut is CTRL-X.

28. The keyboard shortcut for Paste is CTRL-P.

29. Many Internet Service Providers will disconnect you when they do not see you actively sending or receiving information while connected on the Internet.

30. To save connect time, it is often best to write your e-mail before you go online. Start your e-mail program. Choose the "Work Offline" option. If your program starts automatically to dial in, press the cancel option. After you have written your e-mail, then go online and send the message.

31. If you do not understand an option in a Windows dialog box, right-click the option, and in most cases you will see a "What's This?" button. Click on it to get help.

32. If you are viewing the contents of a floppy disk, and then insert a new disk into the floppy drive, you can view its contents by hitting the F5 button. This will refresh the contents of the open floppy disk window. The contents of the old disk will disappear from the window, replaced by the new one.

33. To copy a floppy disk, double-click on the My Computer icon. Right-click on the floppy disk icon. Choose Copy Disk from the pop-up screen.

34. When you see a letter underlined in a menu choice, it means that there is a keyboard shortcut for the item. Holding down the key marked "Alt" and pressing the underlined letter at the same time will produce the same results as clicking the mouse on the word.

35. A hotkey is a key or combination of keys such as CTRL and an alphanumeric character, that activate a pop-up program or cause some other predetermined action to occur.

36. If you pay online by credit card, your transactions will be protected by the Fair Credit Billing Act. Consumers have the right to dispute certain charges and temporarily withhold payment while the creditor investigates them.

37. Keep good records while shopping on the Internet. Print a copy of all purchase orders and confirmation numbers for your records. Read and print all e-mail messages a merchant sends you regarding your transaction.

38. When you enter a chat room, watch quietly in the background until you understand the nature of the conversation. Never give your full name, address, phone number or other personal information to anyone you meet in a chat room. Never reveal your social security number or credit card number to anyone in a chat room.

39. Make it a priority to download new versions of your browser when they are released.

40. When using a search function, a keyword is the word the user wants to find in a document.

41. To run a program effectively, it is best to have the recommended requirements instead of just the minimum requirements. Read carefully the requirements on the outside of the software package.

42. There is an add-on for a portable computer that allows you to use a laptop as both a portable and a desktop computer. It is called a docking station or port replicator. You slip the laptop into the docking station and it allows you to connect to accessories such as a keyboard and monitor.

43. A personal digital assistant (PDA) is a handheld device that is used as a personal organizer. It usually combines telephone and

fax functions with a personal organizer and other computer applications.

44. Do not print from a floppy. It usually takes a long time. It is better to copy the file to your hard drive and print from there.

45. Do not use magnets on or near your computer or floppies. If a magnet gets too close to a floppy or hard disk it will erase it.

46. Look for a printer that has a lot of memory. More memory will allow it to print faster.

47. Surge protectors cannot protect from lightning. In severe weather, unplug the entire computer system from the power and telephone lines to avoid damage to your PC.

48. You can find freeware and shareware at many Internet sites. Freeware programs are free to you. Shareware programs are provided for you to try without a cost. If you like the program, you can pay a small fee to register and continue using the program.

49. You can only cut, copy, and paste one text piece at a time. If you cut two segments in succession and then paste, you lose the first cut segment.

50. Keep your virus protection software up to date. Most virus protection updates are available through online services.

51. To view the date on your desktop, move your mouse cursor over the time displayed in the far right corner of the Taskbar. The date will pop-up.

52. To install Accessibility options, click the Start button, then Control Panel. Double-click Add/Remove Programs, and then click the Windows Setup tab. Select the Accessibility Options check box, click OK, and then follow the instructions.

53. To pick a new color scheme for your desktop, right-click the Desktop, choose Properties, then select the Appearance tab. Click the Scheme drop-down menu and choose a new color scheme.

54. To turn off your modem's speaker, go to the Control Panel and double-click the Modems icon. Click the General tab on the Modems property sheet. Select the appropriate modem. Click the Properties button, click the General tab on this new property sheet, and move the slider control all the way to the left. Then click the OK button on each property sheet.

55. If you want to keep the Calculator handy, you can add it to the Windows StartUp group so it will run automatically at startup. Right-click the shortcut properties for the Calculator to run it minimized on your Toolbar until you need it.

56. Portals and Vortex Sites refer to huge sites that are virtual doorways onto the Web. Portals can serve as one stop shopping sites. Send me an e-mail and I'll tell you the one I like best!

57. If you want to silence your PC, check the Mute All box under the first column in the Volume Control window.

58. You can adjust how quickly characters repeat as you hold down a key. Go to the Control Panel and double-click the Keyboard icon. Select the Speed tab and use the slider to adjust the cursor blink rate.

59. You can close an open window by pressing ALT-F4 instead of using your mouse.

60. Software piracy is the unauthorized copying of software.

61. A pixel is a cluster of colored dots that combine to form images on the computer screen.

62. A high-capacity drive is a floppy disk drive that can hold more information than the average floppy. They are slightly larger than regular floppy disks.

63. Cache is a small amount of computer memory that holds most recently used data.

64. Download only from trusted sources.

65. In a domain name, .com means a commercial (business) web site. School sites have .edu and government sites have .gov endings.

66. Do not delete program files. If you want to get rid of a program, uninstall it.

67. Keys with two characters on them give you the lower character. To get the upper character, press the Shift key.

68. Do not use the lower case L for the number one, or a capital O for zero. The computer is literal and treats them very differently.

69. To scroll continuously, hold the mouse button down instead of just clicking.

70. If you are buying a DVD (digital versatile disc) drive so that you can watch DVD movies on your PC, you need to make sure you have a multimedia computer.

71. When you purchase floppy disks, make sure that they are formatted for a PC. The disk box says they are Windows, IBM, or PC formatted. Do not buy disks formatted for a Mac. They will not work in your machine.

72. Clicking with the left mouse button will select any item. Clicking with the right mouse button will give you information about the item or things that you can do with that item.

73. You can send anything to the Recycle Bin by highlighting it and pressing the Delete key or by dragging it to the Recycle Bin.

74. You can delete a shortcut (icon with a small arrow on it) without in any way affecting the program or folder itself.

75. When you delete files or programs, they stay in the Recycle Bin until you empty it. Items in the Recycle Bin take up space on your hard drive.

76. You can highlight any text or graphic by clicking your mouse on it or clicking the mouse button and holding it down while dragging across your intended selection.

77. You can drag any icon, file, or document to your desktop for quick retrieval. Get into the habit of using your right mouse button to drag items. When dragging with your right

mouse button you are always presented with a choice. The computer will ask if you want to copy, move, or create a shortcut to the item.

78. FAQ stands for Frequently Asked Questions. It is a list of questions and answers you can review to familiarize yourself with the content.

79. Right-clicking your mouse on any icon, file, or folder will give you a useful menu, which has information about the object. This menu allows you to rename or delete the object and also can show you the object's properties.

80. In Windows, you can often do the same thing in several different ways. For instance, to save a file in most programs, click on the Save icon, choose Save from the File menu at the top of the screen, or hold down the CTRL key and the s key, at the same time.

81. If you make changes to a file and save it again (without giving it a new name), the old file will be overwritten and only the file with the changes will remain on the disk.

82. You can drag any icon onto the Start button and drop it there. It will be added to the top of the Start menu so you can access it with two clicks instead of three or four.

83. When you save a file, it is written to whatever disk you choose, i.e. hard disk, floppy disk, etc. In most programs, you choose File, then Save. When the Save dialog box appears, be sure to note where the file is being saved. Click on the down arrow next to the Save In box, to choose exactly where you want to put the file.

84. To avoid repetitive stress injuries sometimes associated with computer use (typing), you can buy a special ergonomic keyboard.

85. Most mail programs allow you to store frequently used addresses in an address book. You then look up the addresses in the address book rather than type them in each time.

86. Be sure to put your backup copies in a safe place away from your computer. In case of some type of catastrophe, you will want our backup copies in a secure location.

87. To rename a shortcut icon, right-click the icon, select the Rename command, type a new name, and press Enter.

88. To stop the screen saver and return to your program, press any key or move the mouse.

89. You can minimize the CD Player window, and the CD will continue to play.

90. If you are having a hard time locating icons on the Desktop, alphabetize them. Right-click the Desktop, Arrange Icons, and choose By Name. You can also arrange the icons by type, size, or date.

91. Dust your computer case and monitor at least once a week. If dust gets into the computer case, you could have problems. Do not use furniture polish on your electronics.

92. A slanted keyboard is easier to type on than a flat one. Most keyboards have adjustable legs on the underside that can be pulled into place so the end of the keyboard is higher.

93. Press ESC to cancel a command. The ESC key, in the upper left corner of your keyboard, lets you cancel commands and stop tasks that are underway.

94. If you need to select an entire paragraph in a document, position your cursor in the middle of the paragraph and triple-click.

95. If you seem to be typing over text instead of inserting new test, you may have depressed the INSERT key. To deactivate INSERT, simply press it again.

96. If you point to an underlined item and it does not turn dark, click the desktop blotter icon (third from the Start button) on the taskbar.

97. If your PC starts to slow down, your hard disk may be too full. If you use more than 85% of your hard disk's space, you may need to get rid of unneeded files, or you may need to add an additional hard disk.

98. In printing, the direction of the paper is called orientation. Portrait means that the paper is taller than it is wide. Landscape means the paper is wider than it is tall.

99. A newsgroup is often called a forum. It is an online discussion group where people exchange ideas about a common interest.

100. Usenet is a worldwide bulletin board system that can be accessed through the Internet or through many online services. It contains thousands of newsgroups.

101. Have some fun! Check out my web site www.theseniorsguide.com

1. The Senior's Guide to Easy Computing
   www.theseniorsguide.com

2. American Association of Retired Persons
   www.aarp.org

3. The Senior Center
   www.senior-center.com

4. Seniors-Online
   www.ageofreason.com

5. Baby Boomer's Headquarters
   www.bbhq.com

6. Graphic Design & Illustration
   www.cricketbow.com

7. The Dilbert Zone
   www.unitedmedia.com/comics/dilbert

8. Habitat for Humanity
   www.habitat.org

9. JewishNet Global Jewish Information Center
   www.Jewishnet.net

10. Klingon Language Institute
    www.kli.org

11. The Old Farmer's Almanac
    www.almanac.com

12. Operation Desert Storm Debriefing Book
    www.leyden.com/gulfwar

13. World War II Missing-In-Action
    www.bentprop.org

14. Astrology
    www.astrologyzone.com

15. The Smithsonian Institute
    www.si.edu

16. American Museum of Natural History
www.amnh.org
17. The Kentucky Horse Park
www.imh.org
18. The National Corvette Museum
www.corvettemuseum.com
19. San Diego Aerospace Museum
www.AerospaceMuseum.org
20. Shareware
www.shareware.com
21. Personality Styles
www.FourFriends.org
22. Kelley Blue Book
www.kbb.com
23. Social Security Online
www.ssa.gov
24. IRS
www.irs.ustreas.gov
25. Investor Guide
www.investorguide.com
26. Kiplinger OnLine
www.kiplinger.com
27. The Investment FAQ
www.invest-faq.com
28. NASDAQ
www.nasdaq.com
29. Yahoo/Finance
www.quote.yahoo.com
30. Smart Money Interactive
www.smartmoney.com

31. Market Guide
    www.marketguide.com
32. Fortune
    www.pathfinder.com/fortune
33. Forbes
    www.forbes.com
34. Financial Times
    www.ft.com
35. Consumer World
    www.consumerworld.org
36. Biz Web
    www.bizweb.com
37. Better Business Bureau
    www.bbb.org
38. Musicals Net
    www.musicals.net
39. Museum of Fine Arts
    www.mfa.org/exhibits
40. Success Principles for Business Owners
    www.abovethelinepress.com
41. Amazon Books
    www.amazon.com
42. Bingo Zone
    www.bingozone.com
43. BarnesandNoble Books
    www.barnesandnoble.com
44. Catalog Link
    www.cataloglink.com/cl/home.html
45. Space News Online
    www.spacenews.com

46. U.S. Patent and Trademark Office
    www.uspto.gov
47. Ben and Jerry's Ice Cream
    www.benjerry.com
48. United States Senate
    www.senate.gov
49. U. S. House of Representatives
    www.house.gov
50. Welcome to the White House
    www.whitehouse.gov
51. Achoo
    www.achoo.com
52. Literary Listening
    www.audible.com/adbl/store/
53. National Hospice Organization
    www.nho.org
54. SleepNet
    www.sleepnet.com
55. 1st Headlines
    www.1stheadlines.com
56. Medical Doctors Online
    www.meddoctor.com
57. American Cancer Society
    www.cancer.org
58. Security Check
    www.symantec.com/securitycheck
59. National Jewish Medical and Research Center
    www.njc.org
60. Vita-Web
    www.vita-web.com

61. Ask the Dietician
    www.dietician.com
62. Administration on Aging
    www.aoa.gov/aoa/pages/agepages/
    exercise.html
63. American Contract Bridge League
    www.acbl.org
64. Better Homes and Gardens Online
    www.bhglive.com/index/shtml
65. Collector Online
    www.collectoronline.com
66. The CraftWEB Project
    www.craftweb.com
67. Winners Publishing
    www.winner.com
68. World Wide Quilting
    www.ttsw.com/MainQuiltingPage.html
69. Wine
    www.wine.com
70. Classic Car Show
    www.classicar.com
71. Epicurious
    www.epicurious.com
72. Geneology Home Page
    www.genhomepage.com
73. Pet Talk
    www.zmall.com/pet
74. The American Kennel Club
    www.aka.org

75. Internet Daily News
    www.tvpress.com/idn
76. The Hollywood Reporter
    www.hollywoodreporter.com
77. C-SPAN
    www.c-span.org
78. The New York Times
    www.nytimes.com/yr/mo/day/news/national
79. PointCast Network
    www.pointcast.com
80. USA Today Nation
    www.usatoday.com/news/digest/ndl.htm
81. National Public Radio Online
    www.npr.org/news
82. The Weather Channel
    www.weather.com
83. Ask An Expert
    www.askanexpert.com/askanexpert
84. Britaanica Online
    www.eb.com
85. Cool Word of the Day
    www.edu.yorku.ca/~wotd
86. MapQuest
    www.mapquest.com
87. AAA Online
    www.aaa.com
88. Travelocity
    www.travelocity.com

89. Microsoft Expedia
    www.expedia.msn.com
90. All Hotels on the Web
    www.all-hotels.com
91. BreezeNet's Guide to Airport Rental Cars
    www.bnm.com/rcar.htm
92. NASCAR Online
    www.nascar.com
93. Town Hall
    www.townhall.com
94. Adventure
    www.adventuretv.com
95. Film Festival Server
    www.filmfestivals.com
96. Movies.com
    www.movies.com
97. U.S. Postal Service
    www.usps.gov
98. Allsports
    www.allsports.com
99. Financial Freedom
    www.finfree.com
100. Veterans News and Information Source
    www.vnis.com
101. The Senior's Guide to Easy Computing
    www.theseniorsguide.com

INDEX

Address Book 19, 167, 170, 171, 194

Applications 26, 70, 106, 188

Arrow Keys 86

Attachments 176

Baud Rate 47

Booting Up 63

CD-ROM 23, 33, 37, 38

Central Processing Unit 19, 29

Chat Room 158

Close 50, 67, 73, 88, 151, 169, 183, 188, 190

Control Panel 105, 108, 110, 189, 190

Cookie 160

CPU 19, 28, 29

CTRL 87

Cursor 41, 75, 76, 86, 189, 190, 196

Cut 75, 76, 93, 185

Defragmenting 122

Delete 75, 87, 96 192

Desktop 55, 56, 189, 195

Desktop Model 22

Dialog Box 89, 90, 96, 99, 103, 109, 123, 185, 194

Disk Drives 33

Domain 140, 145, 152, 166, 191

Dot Matrix 44

Double-Clicking 68

Download 127, 153, 154, 155, 159, 161, 187

Drives 19, 23, 33, 34, 37, 38, 59, 117, 118, 122

DVD 23, 33, 38, 192

Electronic Mail 163

E-Mail 126, 163, 177

INDEX

Emoticons. 179

Etiquette 180

Expansion Slots. 42

Extension 61, 166

File 55, 57, 58, 60, 61,76, 90, 91, 92, 93, 94,
96, 99, 100, 101, 119, 120, 144, 145, 152,
153, 155, 161, 168, 175, 176, 183, 188, 193, 194

File Transfer Protocol. 153

Floppy. 33, 35, 36, 37, 62, 63, 121, 183, 186, 191, 194

Folder 57, 62, 77, 90, 91, 92, 93, 99, 105,
110, 111, 117, 118, 120, 154, 192, 193

FTP. 153

Games. 19, 20, 115, 184

Hard Drive. 32, 33, 36, 63, 121, 122,
154, 160, 175, 188, 192

Hardware. .21, 23, 25, 27, 42, 46

Home Page 143, 148

HTML 144

HTTP. 145, 146

Hyperlink. . . . . !44

Icon. 57, 72, 76, 110, 111, 122, 123,
144, 176, 183, 189, 192, 194, 195, 196

Inkjet. 44

Internet 16, 17, 46, 48, 125, 126, 127, 130, 131,
132, 134, 135, 138, 139, 140, 145, 147, 149, 151,
153, 159, 160, 165, 166, 182, 185, 187, 197, 202

ISP. 132, 134, 137, 141, 165

Keyboard. 19, 23, 40, 41, 50, 74, 158,
184, 185, 186, 188, 194, 196

Laser Printer 44

Mac. 21, 192

INDEX

Megbyte 31

Menu 66, 67, 71, 74, 76, 80, 82, 83,
84, 88, 93, 95, 99, 101, 111, 118, 119, 122,
156, 165, 168, 170, 175, 186, 189, 193, 194

Menu Bar. 67, 83, 84

Modem 46, 47, 132, 133, 141, 165, 189

Monitor 19, 23, 39, 50, 52, 63, 73, 81, 102, 188, 195

Mouse 19, 23, 41, 68, 69, 74, 75, 79, 80, 81,
119, 144, 156, 182, 186, 189, 192, 192, 195

MS-DOS 105, 184

Multimedia 43, 126, 159

Multitasking. 116

My Computer. 57, 91, 95, 96, 117, 118, 122, 123, 186

My Documents 91, 119

Newsgroup 126, 157, 180, 196, 197

NumLock 86

Online Shopping 15, 20

Operating System 21, 25, 27, 54, 63

Personal Computer 19, 21

Plug_in 159

Pointer. 41, 58, 68, 78, 79, 119, 144

Printer 44, 45, 188

Programs. 25, 26, 32, 33, 36, 56, 68, 72, 88,
101, 104, 105, 106, 111, 114, 121, 161,
163, 165, 170, 182, 184, 188, 192, 193, 194

Propeller Head. 17, 23, 24, 37, 48, 64

RAM 130, 135, 165

Recycle Bin 96, 192

Save 30, 76, 88, 180, 193, 194

Save As. 76

INDEX

Scan Disk 122

Screen Saver 102, 103, 195

Scrollbar 81

Search 90, 147, 148, 150, 187

Search Engine 150

Secure Saver 131

Software 25, 26, 191

Spreadsheet 114, 175

Start Button 56, 65, 71, 72, 90, 98, 99, 101, 105,
108, 110, 118, 119, 122, 123, 189, 194, 196

Storage .30, 31, 32, 35, 36, 37, 123

System Box 22, 23, 28, 35, 52

Taskbar 56, 65, 70, 71, 77, 78, 80, 196

Toolbar 67, 147, 149

Tower Model 22

Uniform Resource Locator 145

Virus 161, 189

Volatile Memory 30

Web 49, 71, 72, 126, 131, 138, 139, 141,
143, 144, 145, 147, 148, 150, 151, 156,
158, 160, 165, 190, 200, 201, 203

Web Browser 138

Web Site 142

Window 60, 67, 70, 76, 77, 78, 79, 80, 83, 88,
89, 92, 93, 95, 99, 112, 116, 118, 131, 184, 190, 195

Windows Explorer 96, 105, 118

Word Processor 113

World Wide Web 126, 138